TERRY LEARNS TO FLY

THE ADVENTURES OF TERRY PTERODACTYL
BOOK 3

written by
NANA FERRELL

illustrated by
COURTNEY AKAGI

Phase Publishing, LLC

Seattle, WA

If you purchased this book without a cover, you should be aware that this book is stolen property. It was reported as "unsold and destroyed" to the publisher, and neither the author nor the publisher has received any payment for this "stripped" book.

Text copyright © 2022 by Ferrell Hornsby
Image copyright © 2022 by Ferrell Hornsby

All rights reserved. Published by Phase Publishing, LLC. No part of this book may be reproduced or transmitted in any form, or by any means, electronic or mechanical, including photocopying or recording or by any information storage and retrieval system, without written permission from the publisher.

Phase Publishing, LLC first paperback edition
November 2022

ISBN 978-1-952103-46-9
Library of Congress Control Number 2022949043
Cataloging-in-Publication Data on file.

DEDICATION

To all children who are

learning to "fly" in their own way!

Don't give up!

You can do it!

"But, Mother, I can't fly."

Terry looked at his wings.

He felt sad.

"My wings won't work right."

"Climb up on this little rock," his mother said.

"Maybe that will help."

Terry climbed up on the rock.

He looked down at the ground.

The ground looked very far away.

Terry felt scared.

Terry closed his eyes.

He jumped.

He flapped his wings as hard as he could.

He landed with a thump.

Terry started to cry.

"There, there, Terry," his mother said.

She put her wing around him.

"We all fall down sometimes."

"Why don't you go play with your friends?

"We can try again tomorrow."

Terry smiled. "Okay, Mother."

He was glad he didn't have to try to fly again.

Terry found his friends, Brenda, Sarah, and Earl.

They decided to play Kick the Rock.

They played in the grass next to a cliff.

Earl kicked the rock to Sarah.

She kicked it to Terry.

Terry kicked it hard to Brenda.

It flew over the side of the cliff.

Brenda reached for the rock with her foot.

She stumbled back and fell right over the edge.

"Help me!" Brenda called.

"I can't climb up the cliff.

"It's too high."

Terry looked for a way to help.

Sarah and Earl looked, too.

The cliff was very high.

Terry couldn't fly down.

Sarah and Earl couldn't climb down.

Brenda couldn't climb up.

Terry wanted to help his friend.

But he didn't know how.

Suddenly, Brenda screamed.

"Help!" she cried.

"There's a big dinosaur coming.

"It's got big teeth.

"It's going to eat me!"

Terry didn't think.

He just jumped and flapped his wings.

He flew toward the big dinosaur.

He flew right at its face.

He flapped his wings hard.

The big dinosaur turned and ran away.

"Oh, Terry," Brenda said.

"You were so brave!

"Thank you for scaring that big dinosaur away."

"You're welcome, Brenda," Terry said.

Terry looked at his wings.

"I didn't even think about being scared," he said.

"I just wanted to help you.

"I think that's why my wings worked.

"I think that's why I could fly."

Brenda looked up at the side of the cliff.

She saw Sarah and Earl looking down at her.

"I'm glad you can fly," she said.

"But how am I going to get out of here?"

"I'll fly up and find a way," Terry said.

Terry started flapping his wings and ran

along the ground.

After a few steps, he didn't have to run anymore.

He was flying!

It felt good!

Terry landed near Sarah and Earl.

They looked for something to help Brenda.

They found a long vine.

Terry took the end in his mouth.

He flew back to Brenda.

Terry wrapped the vine around her.

Brenda held onto the vine.

She climbed up while her friends pulled.

When she reached the top, they all cheered.

They all walked home with Brenda.

Terry was glad he had friends who would

help each other.

After that, Terry flew everywhere.

Except when he was playing with his friends,

of course.

THE END

Printed in the USA
CPSIA information can be obtained
at www.ICGtesting.com
LVHW062123171223
766712LV00028B/1793